SILVER DOLLARS

BY MADDIE SPALDING

IN GOD
WE TRUST

2010

The Child's World®
childsworld.com

Published by The Child's World®
1980 Lookout Drive • Mankato, MN 56003-1705
800-599-READ • www.childsworld.com

Photographs ©: Shutterstock Images, cover, 1, 8, 9, 12–13; Rare
Coin Wholesalers/Getty Images News/Getty Images, 5, 20
(top); Steve Lovegrove/Shutterstock Images, 6–7; River North
Photography/iStockphoto, 11; Everett Historical/Shutterstock
Images, 15; Kevin H. Knuth/Shutterstock Images, 17; Sergey
Ryzhov/Shutterstock Images, 18–19; Jordi Delgado/iStockphoto,
20 (bottom); Red Line Editorial, 22

Design Elements: Shutterstock Images; Ben Hodosi/Shutterstock
Images

ISBN 9781503820067
LCCN 2016960502

Printed in the United States of America
PA02336

ABOUT THE AUTHOR

Maddie Spalding writes and
edits children's books. She lives in
Minnesota.

TABLE OF CONTENTS

CHAPTER ONE

WHAT IS A SILVER DOLLAR?

Silver dollars are U.S. coins. They are made from silver and copper. Silver and copper are metals.

Flowing Hair Silver Dollars were first made in 1794.

Morgan Silver Dollars were made between
1878–1904 and again in 1921.

Silver dollars come in many **designs**. The design changes every year. The designs show important events and people in U.S. history.

Lady Liberty

IN GOD
WE TRUST

2010

Year the coin
was made

American Silver Eagle coins are
made every year. Lady Liberty is
on the front.

BACK
"E Pluribus Unum" is the United States motto. It is Latin for "Out of Many, One."
UNITED STATES OF AMERICA
E PLURIBUS
UNUM
1 OZ. FINE SILVER~ONE DOLLAR
Eagle

An eagle is on the back.

CHAPTER TWO

THE HISTORY OF THE SILVER DOLLAR

The United States Mint makes coins. The U.S. Mint is part of the U.S. government.

How is a silver dollar different from other U.S. coins?

The U.S. Mint in Denver, Colorado, makes coins.

Lady Liberty also appeared on the Draped Bust silver dollar.

The first U.S. silver
dollars were **minted**
in 1794. A woman was
on the front. Her name
was Lady Liberty.

The U.S. Mint also made dollar coins from other materials. The Susan B. Anthony dollar was made from copper and nickel in 1979. Susan B. Anthony was on the front. The back of the coin honored the ten-year **anniversary** of the moon landing.

Why do you think Susan B. Anthony was put on a dollar coin?

SUSAN B. ANTHONY fought for women's rights in the United States. Her work helped women win the right to vote in 1920.

CHAPTER THREE

VALUE OF THE SILVER DOLLAR

Silver dollars used to be worth $1. But they are worth much more today. This is because silver dollars are uncommon.

Peace silver dollars were made between 1921–1935.

Silver dollars were removed from **circulation** in 1935. The price of silver was too high. But the U.S. Mint still makes silver dollars. They are sold to people who collect coins.

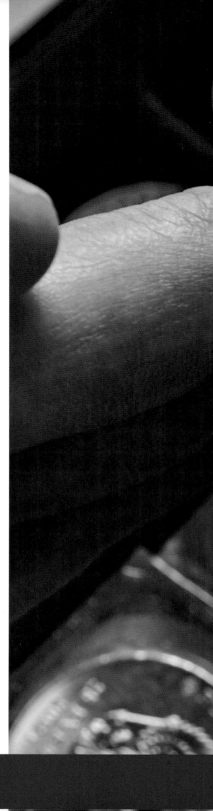

Why might people collect silver dollars?

Silver dollars have nicknames. Some people call them "Ferris wheels."
Others call them "cartwheels."

1794 U.S.
silver dollar

1979 U.S. dollar coin

1794 The first U.S. silver dollars were minted.

1935 Silver dollars were removed from circulation.

1979 Susan B. Anthony first appeared on a dollar coin.

2016 American author Mark Twain first appeared on the silver dollar.

★ The U.S. Mint stopped making silver dollars during the Great Depression. This was a time of financial decline in the United States during the 1930s. Silver dollars were not made between 1935 and 1970.

★ Susan B. Anthony was the first woman other than Lady Liberty to appear on U.S. coins.

★ Other important people who have appeared on silver dollars include Pope Francis and baseball player Jackie Robinson.

★ The 2016 National Park Service silver dollars celebrate U.S. national parks.

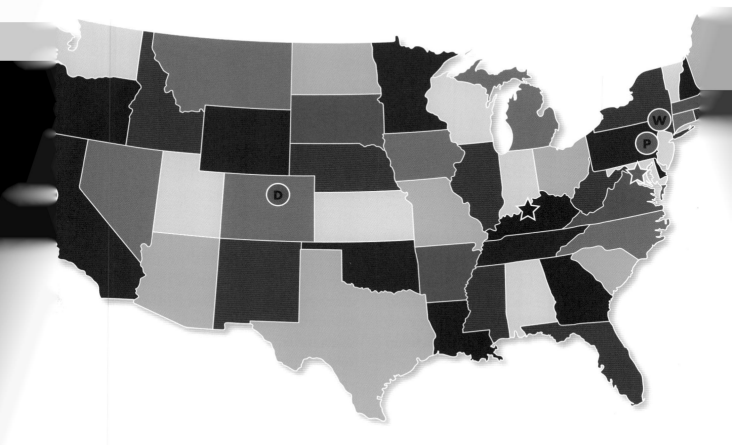

KEY

⭐ Fort Knox, Kentucky—Storage of U.S. gold

⭐ Washington, DC—Headquarters of the U.S. Mint

COIN-PRODUCING MINTS

Ⓓ Denver, Colorado—Produces coins marked with a D.

Ⓟ Philadelphia, Pennsylvania—Produces coins marked with a P.

Ⓢ San Francisco, California—Produces coins marked with an S.

Ⓦ West Point, New York—Produces coins marked with a W.

anniversary (an-uh-VUR-suh-ree) An anniversary is a date people remember because something important happened on that date. The back of the 1979 silver dollar honored the ten-year anniversary of the moon landing.

circulation (sur-kyoo-LAY-shuhn) Money that is in circulation is available to the general public. Silver dollars were removed from circulation in 1935.

designs (di-ZINES) Designs are shapes or styles. Silver dollars come in many designs.

minted (MINT-ed) A coin that is minted is made out of metal. The first U.S. silver dollars were minted in 1794.

IN THE LIBRARY

Dowdy, Penny. *Money.* New York, NY: Crabtree, 2009.

Reid, Margarette S. *Lots and Lots of Coins.*
New York, NY: Dutton, 2011.

Romaine, Claire. *Math with Money.*
New York, NY: Gareth Stevens, 2017.

ON THE WEB

Visit our Web site for links about silver dollars:
childsworld.com/links

Note to Parents, Teachers, and Librarians: We routinely verify our Web links to make sure
they are safe and active sites. So encourage your readers to check them out!

INDEX